CLIMATE CHANGE

Weaving a Sustainable Future: A Roadmap to collective Action in the face of Climate change

Raymond J. Sanchez

Dedication

To the unwavering support and boundless love of my parents who have been the steadfast pillars upon which my dreams have soared. Your encouragement and belief in my journey have been the driving force behind every word penned in this book.

To my well-wishers, whose optimism and cheering voices have echoed in the background of my writing days, providing the motivation needed to overcome challenges and embrace triumphs. Your belief in my creative endeavors has been a source of inspiration that I carry with pride.

And, above all, to the Almighty, the Divine orchestrator of destinies, who granted me the gift of creativity and the opportunity to weave stories. In moments of solitude and uncertainty, your guidance has been my compass, steering me through the labyrinth of imagination.

May the words within these pages be a humble offering of gratitude to those whose love and blessings have illuminated my path. This book is dedicated to the enduring spirits of family, friendship, and the Divine forces that shape our narratives.

Table of Contents

Introduction: A Tapestry of Threads Unraveling

The Earth, once a vibrantly woven tapestry of diverse ecosystems, pulsating with life in a delicate equilibrium, now shows frayed edges, threads pulled loose by an unseen hand. This hand, though, is no phantom; it is our own, the collective grip of humanity, relentlessly squeezing the delicate fabric of our planet. This book delves into the story of this unraveling, exploring the tangled threads of climate change, its stark consequences, and the urgent search for a sustainable future.

Imagine a child holding a glowing globe, a miniature Earth cradled in her tiny hands. Her eyes widen as she watches ice caps shrinking, oceans rising, and forests aflame. This is the future we risk bequeathing to generations yet unborn, a future painted with extreme weather events, mass extinctions, and displacement on a colossal scale. The evidence is irrefutable, etched in melting glaciers, parched landscapes, and the intensified symphony of storms. The scientific consensus is thundering – human activities are warming the planet, unleashing an ecological domino effect that threatens the very web of life we depend on.

But this is not just a story of grim statistics and dystopian predictions. It is a narrative woven with the threads of human resilience, innovation, and the undeniable urge to survive. Across the globe, individuals and communities are rising to the challenge. Farmers are adapting to changing rainfall patterns, architects are designing climate-resilient buildings, and entrepreneurs are harnessing the power of renewable energy. Indigenous communities, stewards of millennia-old knowledge, are leading the way in sustainable land management practices. It is a tapestry of resistance, stitched with grassroots initiatives, bold policy changes, and a growing wave of public demand for action.

However, we cannot ignore the stark reality. The needle is moving on the global thermostat, and time is a luxury we no longer have. Delay and denial are threads woven with complacency, leading us further down a treacherous path. We must face the urgency of this crisis head-on, unraveling the outdated paradigms that perpetuate unsustainable practices. This demands a radical shift in perspective, a transformation from self-serving consumerism to a mindful stewardship of our shared planet. It's about redefining progress, not through endless material accumulation, but through environmental well-being and intergenerational equity.

This book is an invitation to embark on this journey of transformation. We will weave through the complexities of climate science, dissect the intricate tapestry of its impacts, and examine the diverse threads of potential solutions. We will meet the heroes and the skeptics, the victims and the architects of change. We will grapple with thorny questions of policy, economics, and social justice, acknowledging the deep inequalities that exacerbate the effects of climate change.

Ultimately, this book is a call to action, a clarion cry for collective responsibility. It is a tapestry woven with hope, woven with the belief that humanity, the very force that unraveled the first threads, can also become the master weaver, crafting a future where the Earth once again hums with vibrant life, a future where our children can hold a healthy planet in their hands, confident that the tapestry remains whole, the threads of sustainability firmly knitted together.

Turn the page, dear reader, and let us begin this vital conversation. It is time to mend the tapestry, stitch by stitch, act by act, for the sake of our

shared home, and for the generations
to come.

Part I: The Urgency of Our Times

Chapter 1: A Planet in Peril - Unraveling the Tapestry of Our World

The once vibrant palette of our planet, woven with diverse ecosystems teeming with life, now bears the scars of an unraveling. The tapestry of Earth, once taut and vibrant, stretches and strains under the relentless pressure of rising temperatures, surging seas, and the fury of unchained weather. This is not a distant threat whispered in scientific reports; it is a grim reality etched in melting glaciers, parched landscapes, and the crescendo of extreme weather events echoing across the globe. This chapter delves into the heart of this unfolding crisis, the tapestry's fraying edges, and the urgent call for repair.

The Earth's fever is undeniable. The thermometer of our planet, meticulously charted for centuries, now spikes with alarming consistency. Each passing year sets a new record, 2023 blazing hotter than its predecessors. This seemingly small rise, a fraction of a degree on a vast scale, unleashes a cascade of consequences. Ice caps retreat, weeping icy tears as they shrink, contributing to rising sea levels that lap hungrily at the edges of coastal communities. Ocean waters, warming relentlessly, expand like a cauldron, devouring islands and eroding shorelines.

The tapestry of life, intricate and interdependent, unravels with each degree of warming. Coral reefs, pulsating metropolises of marine life, bleach and fade, ghosts of their former brilliance. Forests, once verdant lungs of the planet, ignite in infernos, spewing smoke and ash into the choked sky. Species stumble towards extinction, victims of a changing climate that renders their habitats uninhabitable. The delicate balance of ecosystems, honed over millennia, teeters on the precipice of collapse.

For human populations, the consequences are no less severe. Droughts parch fertile lands, turning agricultural heartlands into dust bowls. Floods, unleashed by erratic rainfall patterns, inundate cities and sweep away livelihoods. The specter of famine stalks millions, as climate change disrupts food production and distribution systems. Heatwaves, once occasional inconveniences, now become deadly marathons, testing the limits of human endurance.

The tapestry of human society, too, feels the strain. Displacement becomes a grim reality, as rising sea levels and extreme weather events force people to flee their homes, carrying the weight of loss and uncertainty. Conflict brews over dwindling resources, water becoming a new gold as rivers run dry and aquifers deplete. The ripple effects of climate change echo through economies, disrupting trade, infrastructure, and the very fabric of social stability.

But amidst the unraveling, a thread of hope emerges. Across the globe, individuals and communities rise to the challenge, weaving new strands of resilience into the tapestry. Farmers adapt their practices, embracing drought-resistant crops and water-harvesting techniques. Architects design climate-proof buildings, shielding them from the fury of storms and floods. Renewable energy, once a niche alternative, blazes a brighter path, powering communities and reducing our dependence on fossil fuels.

Indigenous communities, custodians of generations-old knowledge, share their wisdom, guiding us towards sustainable land management practices that respect the delicate balance of nature. Policymakers, acknowledging the urgency, craft regulations and incentives to push for a greener future. The fight against climate change becomes a tapestry of innovation, collaboration, and unwavering determination.

However, the needle on the global thermostat continues its ominous ascent. Time is not a luxury we can afford; delay and denial are threads woven with complacency, leading us further down a treacherous path. We must act with the urgency the crisis demands, unraveling the outdated paradigms that perpetuate unsustainable practices. This requires a seismic shift in perspective, a transformation from self-serving consumerism to a mindful stewardship of our shared planet. It demands redefining progress, not through endless material accumulation, but through environmental well-being and intergenerational equity.

This book is an invitation to embark on this journey of transformation, to delve into the intricacies of climate change, examine the diverse threads of potential solutions, and confront the stark realities of inaction. We will meet the heroes and the skeptics, the victims and the architects of change. We will grapple with the complexities of policy, economics, and social justice, acknowledging the deep inequalities that exacerbate the effects of climate change.

Ultimately, this book is a call to action, a clarion cry for collective responsibility. It is a tapestry woven with hope, woven with the belief that humanity, the very force that unraveled the first threads, can also become the master weaver, crafting a future where the Earth once again hums with vibrant life, a future where our children can hold a healthy planet in their hands, confident that the tapestry remains whole, the threads of sustainability firmly knitted together.

Chapter 2: The Science is Clear - Unfurling the Threads of Evidence

Beneath the tapestry of climate change lurks a robust and intricate framework – the unwavering science that underpins our understanding of this crisis. In this chapter, we dissect the threads of evidence, weaving together the scientific consensus on human-induced climate change, exploring the role of greenhouse gases, and unraveling the sobering projections for future scenarios painted by the Intergovernmental Panel on Climate Change (IPCC).

The chorus of scientific voices on climate change is clear and resounding. Over 97% of actively publishing climate scientists agree that human activities are the dominant cause of global warming observed since the late 20th century. This consensus, forged in the crucible of peer-reviewed research and meticulous data analysis, stands as a testament to the robustness of the science.

The culprit behind this warming lies in the invisible threads of greenhouse gases, primarily carbon dioxide (CO_2), methane, and nitrous oxide. These gases act like a thermal blanket, trapping heat radiated from the Earth back into the atmosphere, causing a gradual rise in global temperatures. Fossil fuel combustion, deforestation, and industrial processes are the primary weavers of these gases, spewing them into the atmosphere at an unprecedented rate.

The Intergovernmental Panel on Climate Change (IPCC), the world's leading body for the assessment of climate change, acts as a crucial translator of this complex science into actionable insights. Through comprehensive reports, the IPCC painstakingly collates the latest research, analyzes trends, and projects potential future scenarios based on different emissions pathways.

Each IPCC report, a tapestry woven from thousands of research threads, paints a stark picture of the future we face. The latest Assessment Report 6 (AR6), released in 2021, lays bare the consequences of unmitigated emissions. Under a high-emissions scenario, we can expect global temperatures to rise by 4°C or more by the end of the 21st century, unleashing a cascade of catastrophic events. Sea levels could rise by several meters, inundating coastal cities and displacing millions. Extreme weather events, storms, droughts, and floods would become more frequent and intense, wreaking havoc on ecosystems and human communities.

The tapestry of future scenarios also includes threads of hope. AR6 presents pathways to limit warming to 1.5°C or 2°C above pre-industrial levels, scenarios requiring radical and immediate action. These pathways necessitate a rapid transition to renewable energy sources, widespread energy efficiency measures, and the restoration of natural ecosystems like forests, which act as carbon sinks.

The science is clear, the evidence irrefutable. We are not passive observers watching a natural phenomenon unfold; we are the weavers of our own climate destiny. Each ton of CO_2 emitted, each forest cleared, each inaction becomes a thread woven into the tapestry of a bleak future. But within this somber narrative, another thread emerges – the power of human ingenuity and collective action. By embracing the science, acknowledging the urgency, and weaving together solutions, we can still alter the pattern of the tapestry, stitching a future where humanity and nature coexist in harmony.

This chapter is just the beginning of unraveling the science behind climate change. As we delve deeper, we will explore the intricate mechanisms of global warming, dissect the impacts on different regions and ecosystems, and examine the tools and technologies available to weave a sustainable future. But remember, the most crucial thread remains awareness. The more we understand the science, the more equipped we become to act, to raise our voices, and to demand change.

With knowledge as our weapon and collective action as our shield, we can rewrite the narrative of climate change. Let us turn the page and embark on this crucial journey, armed with the unwavering science and a burning desire to weave a brighter future for generations to come.

Chapter 3: Faces of the Crisis - Woven Threads of Loss and Resilience

The tapestry of climate change is not merely a collection of statistics and scientific data; it is woven with the vibrant, heartbreaking threads of human stories. In this chapter, we move beyond the impersonal numbers and meet the individuals and communities bearing the brunt of this crisis, their lives irrevocably altered by droughts, floods, displacement, and resource scarcity.

In the sun-baked plains of Kenya, we encounter Amina, a farmer whose once fertile land has surrendered to a relentless drought. Each withered maize stalk whispers a tale of lost harvests and dwindling food security. Her family, like countless others across the parched landscape, grapples with hunger, their future etched in the cracked earth.

Floodwaters tell a different story in Bangladesh. We meet Fatima, a fisherman whose makeshift shack clings precariously to the rising tide. The river that sustained his family for generations now threatens to devour their very existence. With saline water infiltrating the soil, crops struggle to survive, and the catch dwindles, painting a bleak picture of food insecurity and displacement.

The threads of climate change reach even the icy fingers of the Arctic. We meet Ayana, a young Inuit, whose ancestors navigated the frozen seas for millennia. Now, melting ice makes traditional hunting routes unpredictable, jeopardizing their way of life and cultural identity. Rising sea levels encroach upon their coastal villages, forcing them to contemplate a future away from the land they know and love.

In the bustling megacities like Manila, the face of climate change is one of displacement and vulnerability. Typhoon Haiyan's scars still etch the city's memory, a stark reminder of the fury of extreme weather events. Millions live precariously, their fragile homes perched on hillsides prone to landslides, their lives a constant gamble against the whims of a changing climate.

But the tapestry of climate change also reveals threads of resilience, woven with the tenacious spirit of human communities. In the Andes mountains, villagers defy water scarcity by reviving ancient irrigation techniques, weaving together ingenuity and tradition to secure their future. In the Amazon rainforest, indigenous communities become the guardians of the forests, using their knowledge to protect biodiversity and mitigate the effects of climate change.

Across the globe, individuals rise as champions of change. Young activists like Greta Thunberg ignite a global movement, their voices a rallying cry for action. Farmers embrace sustainable agriculture, nurturing the land while reducing their carbon footprint. Entrepreneurs weave renewable energy solutions, their innovations lighting the path towards a greener future.

The stories we encounter here are not merely individual struggles; they are threads woven into the fabric of our shared humanity. They remind us that the consequences of climate change are not a distant threat, but a lived reality for millions. They challenge us to recognize the inequalities that exacerbate the crisis, with marginalized communities bearing the brunt of its consequences.

These stories also ignite a spark of hope. They reveal the indomitable spirit of human resilience, our capacity to adapt and innovate in the face of adversity. They showcase the power of collective action, the potential for united voices to weave a tapestry of change, a future where environmental well-being and human prosperity exist in harmony.

This chapter is merely a glimpse into the vast tapestry of human experiences shaped by climate change. As we delve deeper, we will encounter additional stories of struggle and resilience, weaving them together to create a powerful narrative that demands our attention. We will delve into the social and economic injustices that fuel the crisis, explore the psychological impacts on individuals and communities, and celebrate the diverse movements working towards a sustainable future.

Ultimately, the human stories of climate change serve as a potent call to action. They compel us to move beyond apathy and denial, to acknowledge the suffering and the resilience, and to demand change. Each story becomes a thread in the tapestry of awareness, urging us to act with urgency and compassion, to ensure that future generations inherit a planet where their stories don't involve loss and displacement, but a flourishing world woven with hope and sustainable life.

Let us turn the page, embrace the human narratives, and together, unravel a future where the faces of climate change tell a different story – one of adaptation, innovation, and unwavering commitment to a shared future for all.

Part II: The Scope of the Challenge

Chapter 4: A Complex Web of Impacts - Untangling the Threads of Disruption

The tapestry of climate change unravels not in singular strands, but in an intricate web of disruptions woven across diverse sectors. This chapter delves into the interconnected threads of consequences, exploring how rising temperatures, changing weather patterns, and resource scarcity impact agriculture, water resources, energy systems, biodiversity, and human health, painting a comprehensive picture of the crisis's reach.

The Withered Harvest: In the fields of agriculture, the changing climate casts a long shadow. Droughts parch fertile lands, transforming vibrant farms into dust bowls. Erratic rainfall patterns, with torrential downpours alternating with extended dry spells, disrupt planting cycles and decimate yields. Rising temperatures push crops beyond their tolerance limits, leaving farmers struggling to adapt to new pest and disease patterns. These disruptions ripple through food supply chains, exacerbating hunger and malnutrition, particularly in vulnerable communities.

The Thirsty Tapestry: Water, the lifeblood of civilizations and ecosystems, becomes a precious commodity in the face of a warming planet. Melting glaciers shrink, glaciers weep tears of vanishing ice, and snowlines retreat uphill, depleting vital freshwater reserves. Groundwater tables plummet as increased evaporation and agricultural demands outpace replenishment. The delicate balance of watersheds tilts, with rivers running dry and coastal aquifers intruded upon by rising sea levels. Water scarcity becomes a source of conflict, as communities compete for the dwindling resource, weaving threads of tension and instability into the tapestry of our world.

The Energy Crossroads: Our modern world, intricately woven with the threads of energy, faces a fundamental shift. Fossil fuels, the traditional workhorses of our energy systems, become the villains in the climate change narrative. Their continued combustion spews greenhouse gases, accelerating the very crisis they power. The search for alternatives intensifies, with renewable energy sources like solar, wind, and geothermal emerging as the threads of a sustainable future. However, the transition necessitates massive infrastructure upgrades, policy changes, and societal shifts, demanding innovative solutions and a collective commitment to decarbonization.

The Unraveling Web of Life: In the tapestry of biodiversity, each species, however minute, plays a vital role. With climate change, this intricate web unravels. Rising temperatures and changing habitats push plants and animals beyond their adaptive limits, triggering extinctions and cascading ecosystem disruptions. Coral reefs, vibrant undersea metropolises, bleach and die, leaving behind ghostly skeletons, a stark reminder of the vulnerability of marine ecosystems. Forests, the lungs of our planet, succumb to wildfires and deforestation, jeopardizing biodiversity and exacerbating climate change. The delicate balance of nature, honed over millennia, hangs precariously on the edge of collapse, posing a threat to the very foundation of life on Earth.

The Threads of Human Health: The tapestry of human health, too, feels the strain of a changing climate. Heatwaves, once occasional inconveniences, become deadly marathons, pushing the human body to its limits. Air pollution worsens with rising temperatures, triggering respiratory illnesses and cardiovascular problems. Waterborne diseases spread as floods contaminate water sources, posing a threat to vulnerable populations. Mental health suffers, with anxiety and depression rising as communities grapple with the uncertainties and losses brought on by climate change. The web of health unravels, revealing the stark inequalities, with marginalized communities often bearing the brunt of the health impacts.

This chapter serves as a stark reminder that climate change is not a sectoral threat; it is a systemic crisis that touches every facet of our existence. The threads of its consequences are woven into the fabric of our daily lives, from the food we eat to the water we drink, the air we breathe, and the environment that sustains us.

However, within this unraveling tapestry, threads of hope remain. Innovations in agriculture, such as drought-resistant crops and water-harvesting techniques, offer the potential for a more resilient food system. Technological advancements in renewable energy accelerate the transition away from fossil fuels. Conservation efforts and the establishment of protected areas strive to mend the frayed edges of biodiversity. The rise of climate-resilient infrastructure and adaptive strategies aim to shield communities from the worst impacts of a changing climate.

The complexity of the interwoven consequences demands a multifaceted approach. Addressing climate change requires not just isolated solutions, but a holistic perspective that tackles the interconnections and vulnerabilities. It necessitates collaboration across sectors, governments, communities, and individuals. It demands scientific innovation, policy changes, and a shift in our values, prioritizing environmental sustainability over short-term gains.

Agriculture: The fields groan under the sun, crops wilting in the relentless heat. This is the story of Aarti, a smallholder farmer in India, facing crop failures and dwindling yields due to erratic rainfall patterns. Her story echoes across the globe, representing the millions struggling with rising temperatures, increasing pests, and water scarcity. Yet, threads of resilience emerge. Drought-resistant crop varieties like sorghum and cassava offer hope, while water-harvesting techniques developed by Kenyan farmers like Mumbua conserve precious drops. Innovation, like vertical farming in Singapore, provides alternative paths to food security. Policy shifts towards sustainable agriculture, as championed by movements like La Via Campesina, advocate for ecological farming practices and fairer trade relations.

Water Resources: In parched lands like Namibia, the Himba people grapple with dwindling water sources. Their story illustrates the global struggle for access to clean water, threatened by declining groundwater levels and saltwater intrusion. Technological advancements like desalination plants offer solutions, but at a cost, raising concerns about equity and affordability. In Brazil, the "Water Guardians" movement, led by indigenous communities, protects watersheds and promotes sustainable water management, demonstrating the power of community-driven solutions. Meanwhile, initiatives like rainwater harvesting in Sri Lanka empower individuals to take control of their water needs.

Energy: The hum of fossil fuels hangs heavy in the air, but the wind whispers of change. In coal-dependent communities like Appalachia, the story is one of transition, facing economic uncertainty amidst the shift towards renewable energy. Yet, solar panels glint on rooftops in Germany, a testament to the growing adoption of renewables. Technological advancements like wind turbines capable of harnessing offshore winds and energy storage solutions are weaving a cleaner future. Policy initiatives like feed-in tariffs and carbon pricing create incentives for renewables, while countries like Costa Rica set ambitious goals for carbon neutrality, demonstrating the path towards a decarbonized world.

Biodiversity: In the silent depths of the Great Barrier Reef, the vibrant corals bleach and fade. This is the story of countless species facing habitat loss, migration disruptions, and extinction due to climate change. Yet, conservation efforts like community-driven coral restoration projects in Indonesia and protected areas like the Yasuni National Park in Ecuador offer hope for vulnerable ecosystems. Technological advancements like drone-based monitoring and genetic engineering provide tools for understanding and protecting biodiversity. Meanwhile, movements like "30x30" advocate for protecting 30% of the planet by 2030, highlighting the critical role of conservation in mitigating climate change and preserving life on Earth.

Human Health: In heatwave-ravaged cities like Delhi, the stories of heatstroke victims weave a tapestry of human vulnerability. Air pollution worsens, and waterborne diseases spread, exacerbating health risks, particularly for marginalized communities. Yet, climate-resilient healthcare infrastructure, like heat stress early warning systems, is being developed. Telemedicine initiatives in remote areas like Alaska provide access to healthcare despite environmental challenges. Community-based education programs, like those led by healthcare workers in Bangladesh, empower individuals to adapt to changing conditions and protect their health.

These are just glimpses into the intricate tapestry of challenges and solutions across sectors. As we delve deeper, we will encounter more inspiring stories, groundbreaking innovations, and policy initiatives weaving a pathway towards a sustainable future. We will explore the ethical considerations and economic consequences of different approaches, advocating for solutions that are equitable and leave no one behind.

Ultimately, unraveling the threads of climate change is not just an intellectual exercise; it is a call to action. By understanding the challenges and solutions in each sector, we can empower ourselves to become agents of change. We can support sustainable practices in our daily lives, advocate for climate-friendly policies, and invest in technologies that offer hope for a healthier planet. Together, we can rewrite the narrative of climate change, weaving a tapestry of resilience, innovation, and collective action that ensures a thriving future for generations to come.

Remember, the book is your canvas. You can choose which specific stories, advancements, and policy initiatives to highlight within each sector, adapting the content to your target audience and focusing on issues relevant to your region or area of expertise. By weaving together diverse threads of knowledge and inspiration, you can create a powerful narrative that compels readers to engage with the challenges and solutions of climate change, leaving them informed, empowered, and hopeful for a brighter future.

Chapter 5: Vulnerability and Inequality - Cracks in the Tapestry of Progress

The tapestry of climate change, though intricately woven, reveals stark fault lines – gaping inequalities in who bears the brunt of its consequences. This chapter delves into the shadows of the narrative, where vulnerability casts long shadows and existing inequalities deepen under the strain of a warming planet. It explores how geography, socioeconomic status, and gender shape the uneven distribution of climate risks and impacts, weaving a story of injustice within the larger crisis.

Geography sculpts the first threads of vulnerability. Island nations like Kiribati face existential threats from rising sea levels, their very land slipping beneath the waves. Communities living in drought-prone regions like the Sahel grapple with food insecurity and water scarcity, the land they depend on turning to dust under the relentless sun. Extreme weather events, from hurricanes in the Caribbean to floods in Bangladesh, disproportionately impact developing countries, their infrastructure and resources inadequate to withstand the fury of nature. The tapestry of geography underscores the reality that location can be a cruel lottery, assigning vulnerability as readily as privilege.

Socioeconomic threads weave another layer of inequality into the climate change narrative. Poverty acts as a multiplier of risk, leaving marginalized communities less able to adapt, recover, and build resilience. In informal settlements with poor housing and sanitation, floods become deadly inundations. Lack of access to healthcare makes communities more susceptible to climate-related illnesses. Limited financial resources restrict options for migration, trapping people in areas prone to disasters. The tapestry of climate change reveals a brutal truth – the poor become poorer, the vulnerable more exposed, as the threads of their well-being unravel under the pressure of environmental crisis.

Gender adds another layer of complexity to the vulnerability tapestry. Women, burdened with traditional roles and limited access to decision-making, are often disproportionately impacted by climate change. In rural communities, they bear the brunt of water scarcity and deforestation, spending hours each day fetching water and collecting firewood.

Climate-related displacement often disrupts traditional social structures, increasing their risk of exploitation and violence. The tapestry of gender inequality shines a light on the need for climate solutions that empower women, recognize their unique vulnerabilities, and ensure their equitable participation in adaptation and mitigation strategies.

The interwoven threads of geography, socioeconomic status, and gender paint a stark picture of climate injustice. This injustice cannot be ignored; it demands action on multiple fronts. Developed nations, historically the largest contributors to greenhouse gas emissions, have a moral imperative to provide financial and technological support to vulnerable communities, aiding in adaptation and resilience building. Climate policies must be just and equitable, avoiding measures that disproportionately burden the poor and marginalized. Empowering women through education, access to resources, and leadership opportunities is crucial for building resilient communities and driving sustainable development.

The vulnerability and inequality woven into the fabric of climate change cannot be erased overnight. However, we can mend the tapestry, stitch by stitch. By acknowledging the disparities, implementing just and equitable solutions, and fostering international cooperation, we can ensure that the burdens of climate change are not borne solely by the most vulnerable. Building a resilient future means leaving no one behind, weaving a tapestry of social justice and environmental sustainability where everyone, regardless of geography, socioeconomic status, or gender, has the opportunity to thrive in a healthy planet.

Understanding the nuances of vulnerability and inequality is not merely an academic exercise; it is a call to action. By recognizing the uneven distribution of risks and impacts, we can mobilize resources, advocate for equitable solutions, and ensure that our efforts to address climate change leave no one behind. Together, we can weave a tapestry of justice and resilience, a future where the threads of geography, socioeconomic status, and gender no longer dictate vulnerability, but empower communities to adapt, thrive, and contribute to a sustainable world for all.

Chapter 6: Geopolitical Shifts - Cracks in the Global Order

The tapestry of climate change casts a long shadow, not just on ecosystems and communities, but on the very fabric of global affairs. This chapter delves into the shifting sands of geopolitics, exploring the ripple effects of a warming planet on international relations, resource competition, climate refugees, and the potential for conflict. As the threads of environmental stress tighten, new power dynamics emerge, alliances are tested, and the stability of the global order hangs precariously in the balance.

A Scramble for Scarcity: Climate change unleashes a race for dwindling resources, weaving threads of tension into the tapestry of international relations. Freshwater, precious and life-sustaining, becomes a source of contention as rivers dwindle and glaciers melt. Countries like Egypt and Ethiopia, locked in a historic tug-of-war over the Nile, face a future where water rights might become a casus belli. Resource-rich regions like the Arctic, once frozen wastelands, become the new Eldorado, with nations jockeying for access to melting ice sheets and newly navigable sea routes. The shadows of resource wars, fought over oil a century ago, loom large on the horizon, raising questions about a future where water replaces black gold as the coveted prize.

The Tide of Humanity: As sea levels rise and extreme weather events intensify, the tapestry of displacement thickens. Millions are cast adrift, not on rickety boats, but on the rising tides of climate change. Communities in low-lying island nations like Tuvalu and Kiribati grapple with the existential threat of their very land disappearing beneath the waves, weaving stories of forced migration and loss of cultural identity. Climate refugees, not fleeing war or persecution, but the wrath of a changing climate, challenge existing legal frameworks and test the capacity of host nations. The tapestry of international cooperation stretches thin, revealing the need for new policies and frameworks to address the rising tide of climate-induced displacement.

Conflict and Chaos: The threads of climate change intertwine with existing geopolitical tensions, weaving a tapestry of potential conflict. Border disputes, simmering for decades, flare into bloody clashes as water scarcity exacerbates resource competition. Droughts and floods destabilize fragile states, creating fertile ground for extremist groups to exploit vulnerabilities. In vulnerable regions like the Sahel, the tapestry of poverty and environmental stress becomes a canvas for conflict, blurring the lines between climate change and traditional drivers of war. The shadows of climate wars, fought not for ideology, but for survival, paint a grim picture of a future where environmental stress becomes a potent trigger for violence and instability.

However, within these shadows of tension and conflict, the tapestry of climate change also reveals threads of hope and cooperation. International initiatives like the Paris Agreement, though challenged by implementation gaps, serve as a testament to the potential for collective action. Regional alliances, like the Mekong River Commission, work to manage shared water resources and address environmental challenges collaboratively. Innovative partnerships, like the Climate Investment Funds, support vulnerable countries in building resilience and transitioning to low-carbon economies. The tapestry of global governance, though frayed, holds the promise of collective action and shared responsibility in mitigating the worst impacts of climate change.

The geopolitical shifts woven by climate change demand a paradigm shift in international relations. Multilateral cooperation, not nationalistic competition, becomes the key to navigating the challenges of a warming planet. Investing in climate diplomacy, building resilience in vulnerable regions, and addressing the root causes of conflict are vital threads in weaving a tapestry of peace and stability. Embracing renewable energy sources and decarbonizing economies reduces resource competition and fosters a collaborative transition to a sustainable future.

Ultimately, the future of geopolitics in the face of climate change remains a tapestry woven with both threats and opportunities. The choices we make today, the alliances we forge, and the resources we invest will determine the pattern of this tapestry. Will we succumb to the tensions and conflicts fostered by environmental stress, or will we rise to the challenge with collective action and shared responsibility? The answer lies in our capacity to unravel the complexities of climate change, recognize its geopolitical implications, and weave a future where cooperation, sustainability, and resilience become

the dominant threads in the tapestry
of international relations.

Chapter 7: Mitigation: Curbing Our Emissions - Weaving a Tapestry of Sustainable Solutions

The tapestry of climate change stretches before us, its threads interwoven with consequences, but there are also threads of hope, threads of action, threads of mitigation. This chapter shines a light on these vibrant strands, showcasing the strategies we can weave to curb our greenhouse gas emissions, unraveling the intricate patterns of change required within various sectors to transition to a sustainable future.

Unfurling the Wind and Sun: Renewable energy emerges as a radiant thread, bright and promising. Wind turbines, like giants dancing in the sky, harness the power of the breeze, weaving electricity from an inexhaustible source. Solar panels, shimmering mosaics across rooftops and fields, capture the sun's kiss, transforming it into clean, silent energy. Hydropower, geothermal, and ocean energy – each thread contributes to the vibrant tapestry of a renewable future. Investing in research and development, expanding infrastructure, and incentivizing adoption through policy and market mechanisms are crucial steps in untangling the knots of fossil fuel dependence and weaving a greener energy grid.

The Efficiency Imperative: Energy efficiency, a thread woven with meticulousness, reduces our demand for energy altogether. From smart appliances that hum with minimal consumption to retrofitting buildings for optimal insulation, each stitch diminishes our reliance on carbon-intensive sources. Promoting efficient technologies, advocating for stricter energy-efficiency standards, and fostering behavioral change become the instruments for weaving a tapestry of resourcefulness, where less becomes more, and every saved kilowatt hour becomes a victory for the planet.

Reimagining Transportation: The rumble of gasoline engines gives way to the silent hum of electric vehicles as the thread of sustainable transportation takes hold. Buses and cars glide on battery power, weaving a cleaner path through city streets. Trains powered by renewable energy become arteries of progress, connecting populations with swift, zero-emission travel. Active transportation, with bicycles and pedestrians reclaiming their rightful place, adds vibrant streaks of health and community to the tapestry. The challenge lies in building charging infrastructure, ensuring equitable access, and investing in public transportation, but the rewards are clear – cleaner air, quieter streets, and a future where the only fumes we breathe are the scent of progress.

Protecting the Trees, Preserving the Breath: In the emerald tapestry of forests, every leaf whispers the story of life. Yet, deforestation unravels this vital fabric, releasing stored carbon and disrupting ecosystems. Sustainable forest management, community-driven conservation initiatives, and robust anti-deforestation policies become the tools for mending the tears. Weaving together protected areas, agroforestry practices, and innovative solutions like REDD+ (Reducing Emissions from Deforestation and Forest Degradation) offers a chance to ensure forests remain the lungs of our planet, breathing life into a sustainable future.

The threads of mitigation, though diverse, are intricately interconnected. Transitioning to renewable energy reduces reliance on fossil fuels, fostering research and development that benefits sustainable transport. Energy efficiency measures decrease demand, creating opportunities for investing in renewable infrastructure. Protecting forests not only preserves biodiversity but also acts as a carbon sink, reducing the burden on other mitigation strategies. Each thread strengthens the others, weaving a resilient tapestry of solutions that tackles climate change on multiple fronts.

The transition to a low-carbon future is not without its challenges. Technological advancements need acceleration, infrastructure requires significant investment, and societal mindsets need to shift. However, the costs of inaction are far greater – rising sea levels, extreme weather events, and disruptions to ecosystems and economies. The tapestry of mitigation offers not just a solution, but an opportunity – an opportunity to create jobs in green industries, improve public health by reducing air pollution, and build a more equitable and sustainable future for generations to come.

Investing in renewable energy research and infrastructure, implementing strong energy efficiency policies, promoting sustainable transportation options, and protecting forests are not mere threads; they are the foundation stones of a new paradigm. This paradigm, woven with innovation, commitment, and collective action, holds the promise of a world where the tapestry of climate change is no longer a narrative of despair, but a testament to our ingenuity, resilience, and unwavering commitment to the health of our planet and ourselves.

Ultimately, the journey towards a low-carbon future is not merely an academic exercise; it is a call to action. By understanding the diverse threads of mitigation and recognizing the urgency of the challenge, we can become agents of change. We can advocate for policies that support sustainable practices, invest in solutions that benefit our communities and the planet, and inspire others to join the tapestry of collective action.

Chapter 8: Adaptation: Living with the Changes - Weaving Resilience amidst the Threads of Uncertainty

The tapestry of climate change reveals not just threads of disruption, but also threads of resilience. This chapter delves into the realm of adaptation, exploring the strategies we can weave to live with the inevitable impacts of a warming planet. From resilient infrastructure to climate-smart agriculture, early warning systems to disaster preparedness, each thread becomes a strand of hope, a testament to our ability to bend with the wind and find strength in flexibility.

Building for the Future: The thread of resilient infrastructure runs strong and steel-forged. Seawalls rise against rising tides, protecting coastal communities from the encroaching ocean. Flood-proof buildings, designed to weather storms, stand as sentinels against extreme weather. Water management systems adapt to changing rainfall patterns, ensuring access to life-giving water even in times of drought. Investing in resilient infrastructure becomes a strategic stitch in the tapestry of adaptation, protecting lives, livelihoods, and economies from the inevitable impacts of climate change.

Cultivating Change in the Fields: The thread of climate-smart agriculture takes root in fertile fields and verdant farms. Drought-resistant crops, tailored to withstand arid conditions, nourish communities facing water scarcity. Diversified cropping systems, mimicking nature's wisdom, build resilience against pests and diseases. Agroforestry practices, weaving trees into agricultural landscapes, sequester carbon and conserve soil. By embracing innovation and adapting traditional practices, farmers become weavers of resilience, ensuring food security in a changing climate.

Forewarned is Forearmed: The thread of early warning systems hums with the urgency of preparedness. Satellite technology watches from above, tracking storms and predicting floods. Floodplain mapping warns communities of potential dangers, guiding evacuation efforts and minimizing loss. Robust communication networks spread awareness through every channel, ensuring timely alerts reach even the most vulnerable populations. Early warning systems stitch together threads of data, technology, and communication, empowering communities to prepare for the inevitable, transforming threats into opportunities for proactive action.

Readying for the Storm: The thread of disaster preparedness runs through communities, weaving them into a web of solidarity. Evacuation plans, practiced and meticulously crafted, ensure swift and safe relocation when danger comes knocking. Emergency stockpiles, filled with food, water, and medical supplies, stand ready to support those in need. First responders, trained and equipped, become the guiding hands amidst the chaos, stitching together the broken threads of normalcy after disaster strikes. By preparing together, communities become tapestries of resilience, their collective strength woven from preparedness, compassion, and a shared determination to rebuild.

The tapestry of adaptation is not without its challenges. Funding for infrastructure is critical, particularly in vulnerable developing countries. Equitable access to climate-smart agriculture technologies and early warning systems remains a hurdle. Building capacity, raising awareness, and fostering community leadership are crucial for effective disaster preparedness. Yet, despite these challenges, the threads of adaptation offer a narrative of hope and resilience.

By investing in sustainable infrastructure, promoting climate-smart agriculture, implementing robust early warning systems, and fostering a culture of preparedness, we can build a future where climate change, though an ever-present force, does not dictate our fate. We can empower communities to thrive in a changing environment, weaving stories of adaptation into the larger tapestry of human resilience.

Ultimately, the journey of adaptation is not a solitary venture; it is a collective endeavour. By understanding the diverse threads of resilience, sharing knowledge and resources, and working together across borders and communities, we can weave a future where human ingenuity and unwavering commitment overcome the challenges of a changing climate. With each stitch of adaptation, we build not just resilience, but hope, weaving a tapestry where humans and nature, though forever entangled in the dance of climate change, learn to adapt, thrive, and coexist in a sustainable and resilient world.

Chapter 9: Transformation: Rethinking our Relationship with the Planet - Weaving a New Paradigm from the Threads of Change

The tapestry of climate change stretches before us, its threads a grim testament to our unsustainable relationship with the planet. Yet, woven within this narrative are also threads of hope, shimmering threads of transformation, beckoning us to rewrite the story. This chapter delves into the realm of systemic change, advocating for a radical shift in our values, systems, and behaviors, weaving a new paradigm where sustainability and harmony with nature form the warp and woof of our existence.

Circular Economy: Closing the Loop: The thread of the circular economy disrupts the linear model of "take, make, waste." It envisions a closed loop, where resources are endlessly recycled, reused, and repurposed. From upcycling discarded materials to extending product lifespans through repair and refurbishment, the circular economy stitches together threads of efficiency, innovation, and resource conservation. By rethinking how we design, produce, and consume, we can break free from the shackles of unsustainable resource extraction and waste generation, weaving a tapestry of circularity where every object holds the potential for a new life.

Degrowth: Less can be More: The thread of degrowth challenges the dominant paradigm of endless economic growth. It advocates for a deliberate shift towards a state of steady-state or even controlled reduction in material consumption and energy use. This may seem counterintuitive, but degrowth proposes that true progress lies not in accumulating more, but in living well within the planet's ecological boundaries. By prioritizing well-being, sustainability, and community over GDP growth and material acquisition, we can weave a tapestry of a fulfilling and equitable future where "enough" is more than enough.

Beyond Consumption: Rethinking Values: The thread of value redefinition runs deep within the tapestry of transformation. It dismantles the equation of happiness with material possessions and limitless consumption. It embraces simplicity, sufficiency, and the pursuit of non-material values like community, environmental stewardship, and personal growth. By deconstructing societal narratives that drive overconsumption and prioritizing intrinsic over extrinsic rewards, we can weave a tapestry of human flourishing where experiences, relationships, and a connection to nature become the primary currencies of fulfillment.

Sustainable Development: Weaving Equity and Ecology: The thread of sustainable development binds together environmental protection, social equity, and economic prosperity. It envisions a future where development meets the needs of the present without compromising the ability of future generations to meet their own. This demands a holistic approach that addresses climate change while tackling poverty, inequality, and human rights concerns. By prioritizing the needs of vulnerable communities and ensuring inclusive governance, we can weave a tapestry of sustainable development where progress benefits all, leaving no one behind in the transition to a greener future.

The tapestry of transformation is not without its challenges. Shifting from a growth-oriented economy to a steady-state model requires profound economic and societal shifts. Rethinking values and embracing degrowth principles challenge deeply ingrained cultural norms and consumerist patterns. Ensuring equitable access to sustainable solutions and addressing the needs of vulnerable communities during the transition are critical considerations. Yet, despite these challenges, the threads of transformation offer a path towards a future where we live in harmony with the planet and each other.

Investing in research and development for circular economy technologies, creating policy frameworks that incentivize resource efficiency and discourage waste, and fostering cultural shifts that celebrate minimalism and sustainable living are crucial stitches in the tapestry of change. Embracing degrowth principles through shorter working weeks, universal basic income, and localized economies reduces environmental pressure and allows individuals to pursue meaningful lives beyond the treadmill of relentless consumption. Redefining our values requires education, awareness campaigns, and community-driven initiatives that promote mindful consumption, prioritize experiences over possessions, and celebrate our connection to nature.

Ultimately, the transformation we need is not merely a technical or economic endeavor; it is a revolution of the mind and spirit. By rewriting our narrative of progress, rethinking our relationship with the planet, and embracing the threads of a sustainable future, we can weave a tapestry of hope, resilience, and shared responsibility. In this tapestry, humans are not masters of the planet, but co-creators, living in harmony with nature, guided by values of simplicity, equity, and respect for all living beings. This is the transformation we must choose, the story we must write, the tapestry we must weave together, stitch by stitch, thread by thread, for the sake of ourselves and generations to come.

Chapter 10: The Power of Collective Action - Weaving a Tapestry of Change, Thread by Thread

The tapestry of climate change stretches across borders, continents, and communities, its threads interwoven with challenges that no single nation can overcome alone. This chapter delves into the vibrant and dynamic realm of collective action, illuminating the critical roles played by international cooperation, national policies, and local initiatives in addressing this global crisis. It weaves a narrative of hope and empowerment, demonstrating how, by uniting our efforts across scales, we can craft a future of resilience and sustainability.

Global Tapestry: The Paris Agreement and Beyond: The thread of international cooperation shines brightly in the tapestry of climate action. The Paris Agreement, a landmark pact inked by nations across the globe, stands as a testament to the power of collective will. By setting ambitious goals for emissions reduction, establishing frameworks for financial and technological support, and fostering collaboration among nations, the Paris Agreement offers a roadmap towards a low-carbon future. However, its effectiveness hinges on unwavering commitment, robust implementation plans, and ensuring equity in addressing the burdens and benefits of climate action. Weaving stronger national policies into the global tapestry, ensuring accountability, and supporting vulnerable nations in their transition are crucial stitches in building a truly resilient future.

National Threads: Policies that Shape Change: The thread of national policies runs strong within the tapestry of climate action. Carbon pricing mechanisms, renewable energy incentives, and ambitious emissions reduction targets at the national level create the necessary framework for systemic change. Investing in green infrastructure, promoting sustainable land-use practices, and protecting forests contribute significantly to mitigating climate impacts and building resilience. Each nation, weaving its own thread of policy, contributes to the larger fabric of global progress. Sharing best practices, learning from each other's successes and challenges, and fostering international cooperation in technology transfer and policy development strengthen the collective tapestry, ensuring no nation is left behind in the transition to a sustainable future.

Local Voices, Global Reach: The Power of Community Action: The thread of local initiatives hums with the energy of grassroots movements and community engagement. From community gardens and energy cooperatives to sustainable transportation initiatives and climate education programs, local action forms the vibrant foundation of global change. Empowering communities, providing resources and funding, and celebrating local successes weave a tapestry of ownership and participation in addressing climate challenges. By connecting local efforts to national and international frameworks, and ensuring equitable access to resources and opportunities, we create a symphony of collective action where every voice, every action, contributes to the larger narrative of transformation.

The tapestry of climate action is not without its challenges. Geopolitical tensions can hamper international cooperation. Implementing ambitious national policies requires political will and overcoming vested interests. Ensuring inclusivity and equity in local initiatives demands attention to social justice and marginalized communities. Yet, within these challenges lie opportunities for innovation, collaboration, and resilience. Fostering dialogue and trust between nations, building effective governance frameworks, and supporting community-driven solutions that address local needs and priorities are crucial stitches in strengthening the tapestry of collective action.

The power of collective action lies in its transformative potential. By uniting across borders, weaving together national policies with local initiatives, and amplifying the voices of communities, we can create a future where climate change is not a story of despair, but a narrative of shared responsibility, collaborative action, and a unwavering commitment to a sustainable future for all. This future begins with a choice – to act together, thread by thread, nation by nation, community by community, and weave a tapestry of hope, resilience, and a thriving planet for generations to come.

Chapter 11: Empowering Individuals and Communities - Weaving Threads of Change from the Grassroots Up

The tapestry of climate change stretches broad, its threads entangling nations, ecosystems, and individual lives. Yet, within this narrative of challenge lies a vibrant strand of agency - the power of individuals and communities to rise as agents of change, weaving threads of personal and collective action into the fabric of a sustainable future. This chapter delves into the realm of individual and community empowerment, offering practical guidance on how we can reduce our carbon footprint, advocate for climate policies, and build resilience in the face of a changing planet.

Unraveling the Footprint: Each of us holds a thread, an individual carbon footprint, woven into the larger tapestry of global emissions. Reducing our footprint becomes the first stitch in weaving a story of personal responsibility. Simple actions, like switching to energy-efficient appliances, opting for sustainable transportation, and embracing conscious consumption, contribute to a collective decrease in demand for fossil fuels and environmental destruction.

Implementing mindful practices in our daily lives, from reducing food waste to choosing greener products, sends ripples of positive change across the wider fabric of society.

Raising the Voice: Advocacy forms another vital thread, woven through community engagement and policy action. Joining climate groups, writing to elected officials, and participating in peaceful demonstrations amplifies the collective voice, ensuring that the concerns of individuals are heard within the halls of power. Supporting climate-friendly policies through informed voting and public campaigns adds further strength to the tapestry of change. By raising our voices together, we ensure that policymakers prioritize climate action and invest in solutions that benefit our planet and our communities.

Building Resilience: The threads of community resilience shimmer with strength and preparedness. From participating in local tree-planting initiatives to supporting sustainable agriculture projects, individuals can contribute to building stronger, more resilient communities. Learning basic disaster preparedness skills, ensuring access to clean water and emergency supplies, and fostering social networks of support become crucial stitches in preparing for the inevitable impacts of climate change. By working together, sharing knowledge, and building local capacity, communities can navigate the challenges of a changing climate with greater adaptability and collective strength.

The tapestry of individual and community action is not without its challenges. Overcoming apathy, navigating complex policy landscapes, and building community-driven initiatives require dedication, persistence, and resourcefulness. Yet, within these challenges lie opportunities for innovation, collaboration, and personal growth. Embracing peer-to-peer learning, utilizing technology for advocacy and resource sharing, and celebrating small victories become the tools for weaving a resilient and vibrant community fabric.

Ultimately, the power of individual and community action lies in its transformative potential. By taking steps to reduce our footprints, raising our voices for change, and building resilience within our communities, we become agents of positive transformation. This collective force, woven from countless threads of action and commitment, becomes the driving force for a sustainable future. It is a future where individuals are not mere witnesses to climate change, but active participants in shaping a different story, a narrative of hope, responsibility, and collective action.

Together, let us weave a future where the threads of individual and community action become the heart and soul of a sustainable world. It is a future where individual choices matter, where communities thrive in the face of challenges, and where collective action becomes the cornerstone of a world in harmony with the planet and ourselves.

Chapter 12: A Roadmap for Hope - Weaving a Tapestry of a Sustainable Future

The tapestry of climate change stretches before us, its threads interwoven with stories of loss, disruption, and uncertainty. Yet, woven within this narrative lies a vibrant strand of hope – the indomitable human spirit, our capacity for innovation, and the power of collective action to rewrite the future. This final chapter serves as a beacon, illuminating a roadmap for hope, a guide on how we can weave a tapestry of a sustainable future, stitched with resilience, ingenuity, and unwavering commitment.

Our journey through this book has exposed the intricate patterns of the climate challenge. We have delved into the complexities of emissions and mitigation, grappled with the threads of resource scarcity and geopolitical shifts, and explored the paths of adaptation and transformation. Throughout this exploration, one truth has remained constant – the power of human agency, our ability to rise above challenges and become weavers of a better future.

This tapestry of hope begins with a bold embrace of **optimism**. The challenges we face are immense, but so is our capacity for innovation and collaboration. History is our witness – from overcoming pandemics to conquering scientific mysteries, humanity has risen to every challenge, evolving and adapting with relentless creativity. This very essence of human ingenuity is the fertile ground where solutions will bloom.

The first stitch in this tapestry is **individual action**. Each of us holds a thread, a chance to reduce our carbon footprint, champion sustainable practices, and inspire others. From conscious consumption to community outreach, these seemingly small actions, woven together, form a powerful force for change. Every watt of energy saved, every mindful choice made, every voice raised in advocacy adds momentum to the movement towards a sustainable future.

The second stitch is **collective action**. We are not islands in this storm; we are a tapestry woven from communities, nations, and generations. Our strength lies in unity, in collaborating across borders and backgrounds to share knowledge, resources, and solutions. International agreements like the Paris Agreement become the scaffolding on which we build, while community initiatives and grassroots movements form the vibrant heart of this collective endeavor. By uniting our voices, sharing our skills, and supporting each other through challenges, we become an unstoppable force for positive change.

The third stitch is **embracing innovation**. The tapestry of a sustainable future cannot be woven with yesterday's tools. We need game-changing technologies, revolutionary policies, and disruptive solutions that break free from outdated paradigms. Investing in renewable energy research, fostering green technology and infrastructure, and supporting entrepreneurial ventures become crucial steps in weaving a future powered by clean energy and resource efficiency.

The fourth stitch is **building resilience**. The impacts of climate change are already being felt, and they will continue to evolve. Adapting to a changing environment requires agility, foresight, and a commitment to protect the most vulnerable. From strengthening infrastructure to diversifying food systems, investing in social safety nets, and prioritizing ecosystem restoration, we must weave a tapestry of resilience that protects communities, sustains biodiversity, and equips us to navigate the challenges of a new era.

Finally, the most fundamental stitch of all is **hope**. It is the fuel that drives our actions, the light that guides us through darkness, and the unwavering belief that a better future is not just possible, but inevitable. By nurturing hope, we create the fertile ground for positive change, inspiring ourselves and others to take action, collaborate, and persevere.

The tapestry of a sustainable future is not yet complete. The threads are still being spun, the patterns are emerging, and the colors are yet to fully bloom. But with each stitch of individual action, collective effort, innovation, resilience, and hope, we weave a future where humanity thrives in harmony with the planet. This is not a utopian dream; it is a roadmap painted with the colors of possibility, a call to action for every single one of us.